Trains Work Hard

By Sara Lentz

Scott Foresman
is an imprint of

Glenview, Illinois • Boston, Massachusetts • Chandler, Arizona •
Upper Saddle River, New Jersey

Trains carry people.

Trains carry bicycles.

Trains carry animals.

Trains carry oil.

Trains carry cars.

Trains carry logs.

Trains carry coal.